WILFRED OW

Collected ... aphy, were
... in 1998. His other books ... *d Owen:*
... *mplete Poems and Fragments*, and two biographies:
... *Owen* (which won the Duff Cooper Memorial Prize,
... H. Smith Literary Award and the E. M. Forster Award)
... *is MacNeice* (which won the Southern Arts Literary
... He is a Senior Research Fellow of Wolfson College,
... , and a Fellow of the British Academy.

WILFRED OWEN

Poems selected by

JON STALLWORTHY

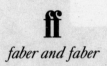

faber and faber

First published in 2004
by Faber and Faber Limited
3 Queen Square London WC1N 3AU

Photoset by Wilmaset Ltd, Birkenhead, Wirral
Printed in England by Bookmarque Ltd, Croydon

Poems © The Executors of Harold Owen's Estate, 1963 and 1983
Introduction and selection © Jon Stallworthy, 2004

The right of Jon Stallworthy to be identified as editor
of this work has been asserted in accordance with
Section 77 of the Copyright, Designs and Patents Act 1988

A CIP record for this book
is available from the British Library

ISBN 0–571–20725–1

10 9 8 7 6 5 4 3 2 1

Contents

Introduction

When, on New Year's Eve 1917, Wilfred Owen proudly told his mother 'I am a poet's poet', he spoke more truly than he knew. He meant, as he wrote, that he was 'held peer by the Georgians', poets associated with the *Georgian Poetry* anthologies edited by Edward Marsh. His work had been praised first (and for him most importantly) by Siegfried Sassoon, and then by Robert Graves and Harold Monro.

We can see him now as 'a poet's poet' in two other senses, only one of which he would have recognized. As a boy, he had bound himself apprentice to a Master, John Keats, and by close study and emulation grafted his own early work on to the Romantic tradition. It was a fortunate – not to say inspired – choice, because he and Keats had more in common, in terms of temperament and talent, than he could have known. Owen warmed to the sensuality and musicality of the older poet, and Keats's physicality (heightened by his study of anatomy and experience of illness) accorded with his apprentice's own precocious awareness of the human body. Owen's earliest extant poem, 'To Poesy' (written in 1909–10), owes much to the theme and diction of Keats's 'The Fall of Hyperion' and speaks of arms, face, eyes, hands, heart, tongue, brow, brain. 'Uriconium' (written in 1913) anticipates even more clearly the tender physicality of Owen's mature work. Porphyro, in Keats's 'Eve of St Agnes', had 'set a table' with delicacies for the sleeping Madeline. This would seem to be subconsciously recalled by the twenty-year-old Owen contemplating the excavated ruins of the Roman city of Uriconium which, with its inhabitants (his guidebook told him), 'perished by fire and sword':

> For here lie remnants from a banquet table –
> Oysters and marrow-bones, and seeds of grape –
> The statement of whose age must sound a fable;

And Samian jars, whose sheen and flawless shape
    Look fresh from potter's mould.
Plasters with Roman finger-marks impressed;
Bracelets, that from the warm Italian arm
    Might seem to be scarce cold;
And spears – the same that pushed the Cymry west,
Unblunted yet ...

Owen's compassionate awareness of the victims' *bodies* – so prominent a feature of his later and greater poems – enables him to feel those

Plasters with Roman *finger-marks* impressed;
Bracelets, that from the *warm Italian arm*
    Might seem to be *scarce cold*;

and it sharpens his perceptions of the weapons that killed them – spears '*unblunted* yet'.

A priggish and self-centred child had, by 1913, grown into a compassionate young man; a transformation encouraged by a second apprenticeship to a second Romantic poet. Two years earlier, while working as a lay assistant to the Vicar of Dunsden, Owen had come upon the poems of Shelley and soon discovered, as he delightedly told his sister,

That Shelley lived at a cottage within easy cycling distance from here. And I was very surprised (tho' really I don't know why) to find that he used to 'visit the sick in their beds; kept a regular list of the industrious poor whom he assisted to make up their accounts;' and for a time walked the hospitals in order to be more useful to the poor he visited! I *knew* the lives of men who produced such marvellous verse could not be otherwise than lovely, and I am being confirmed in this continually.

Owen's devout and devoted mother hoped that her son's experience of Dunsden might lead to a career in the Church. He was to help the Vicar with his parish duties, in return for free board and lodging and some tuition to prepare him for the university entrance exam. The arrangement was not a success. The Vicar had no interest in literature, and Owen soon lost interest in theology, the only topic offered for tuition. Disillusioned, too, by what he called 'The Vicar's Strong Conservatism', he was forced to recognize that literature meant more to him than evangelical religion. This had to be explained to the Vicar. They quarrelled and, in February 1913, Owen left Dunsden on the verge of a nervous breakdown. That summer he sat a scholarship exam for University College, Reading, but failed, and in mid-September crossed the Channel to take up a part-time post teaching English at the Berlitz School in Bordeaux. Over the next two years, he grew to love France, its language and its literature, and had reached perhaps the highest point of happiness that life would offer him, tutoring an eleven-year-old French girl in her parents' Pyrenean villa, when, on 4 August 1914, Germany invaded Belgium and war was declared.

The following month, he wrote to his mother:

I feel my own life all the more precious and more dear in the presence of this deflowering of Europe. While it is true that the guns will effect a little useful weeding, I am furious with chagrin to think that the Minds which were to have excelled the civilization of ten thousand years, are being annihilated – and bodies, the product of aeons of Natural Selection, melted down to pay for political statues.

Those sentiments and the insensitive imagery of *deflowering*, *weeding*, *melted down* show a reversion to Owen's earlier self-regarding priggishness, but a visit to a hospital for the wounded soon brought him to his senses. A September letter to his brother Harold reveals the compassionate concern for the bodies of victims evidenced in his poem 'Uriconium':

One poor devil had his shin-bone crushed by a gun-carriage wheel, and the doctor had to twist it about and push it like a piston to get out the pus. Another had a hole right through the knee [...]

For a year Owen debated with himself whether or not to risk the 'melting down' of his own body. He considered joining the French Army; then contemplated applying for a Commission in the (British) Artists' Rifles; then thought he would 'like to join the Italian Cavalry; for reasons both aesthetic and poetical'. His delayed decision indicates an understandable reluctance to go to war, but at no point do his letters speak of any principled aversion to fighting. 'Do you know what would hold me together on a battlefield?' he asked his mother. 'The sense that I was perpetuating the language in which Keats and the rest of them wrote!' Finally, returning to England with two boys he had been tutoring in Mérignac, near Bordeaux, he said goodbye to his family and, on 21 October 1915, enlisted in the Artists' Rifles.

The following June, Owen was commissioned into the 5th Battalion of the Manchester Regiment, which in January 1917 was thrown into the battle of the Somme. He was engaged in fierce fighting until May, when he was found to be suffering from shell-shock and invalided back to Craiglockhart War Hospital, on the outskirts of Edinburgh. There he met Sassoon and, with his advice and encouragement, began writing the poems that would constitute his own powerful contribution to 'the language in which Keats and the rest of them wrote'. Discharged from Craiglockhart in November 1917, he returned to France in August 1918. He won the Military Cross in a successful assault on the Germans' Beaurevoir–Fonsomme line, but was killed on 4 November, attempting to lead his company across the Sambre and Oise Canal. A week later, the Armistice bells were ringing in Shrewsbury when his parents' front-door bell sounded its small chime, heralding the telegram they had dreaded for two years.

There is a second sense in which Owen is a 'poet's poet'. W. H. Auden, in his great elegy 'In Memory of W. B. Yeats', wrote:

The words of a dead man
Are modified in the guts of the living.

And surely no aspect of Owen's afterlife would have pleased him more than the way his words have been modified in the guts of living poets and contributed to the poetry that came after him. Siegfried Sassoon and Edith Sitwell edited the first edition of his poems that appeared in 1920. More influential was Edmund Blunden's edition of 1931 – influential, in that it was this edition that was read, marked, learnt, and inwardly digested by the next generation of poets, those who would be known as 'the Poets of the Thirties'.

The first to respond in print to Owen was almost certainly Auden, who ended a poem of 1933:

The Priory clock chimes briefly and I recollect
I am expected to return alive
My will effective and my nerves in order
    To my situation.
'The poetry is in the pity', Wilfred said,
And Kathy in her journal, 'To be rooted in life,
    That's what I want.'
These moods give no permission to be idle,
For men are changed by what they do;
And through loss and anger the hands of the unlucky
    Love one another.

There are two quotations from Owen here: the first, his assurance (to his mother) of 4 October 1918, 'My nerves are in perfect order'; the second, a famous statement from the draft Preface to his poems (see page 63) that would be repeated over the years like a mantra, a passage of scripture: 'The poetry is in the pity'.

It was clearly Owen's example – the poet as witness to the horrors of war – that led to Auden's decision trumpeted in a banner headline of the *Daily Worker* on 12 January 1937: 'FAMOUS POET TO DRIVE AMBULANCE IN SPAIN.' Explaining his decision to a friend, Auden wrote: 'I shall probably be a bloody bad soldier but how can I speak to/for them without becoming one?' This echoes a letter of Owen's to his mother: 'I came out in order to help these boys – directly, by leading them as well as an officer can; indirectly, by watching their suffering that I may speak of them as well as a pleader can.' In the event, Auden did not stay long in Spain. He was horrified by what he saw, particularly the burnt-out churches, and the one poem he wrote, overtly, about the Spanish Civil War owes nothing to Owen.

Stephen Spender was more impressionable. His critical book, *The Destructive Element* (1935), shows him to be deeply influenced by Owen. He repeats 'The poetry is in the pity' twice and compares Owen's poems with those of Yeats and Eliot – to the younger poet's advantage. Spender also went to Spain, where he helped the Republicans with radio propaganda and wrote poems such as 'The Coward' and 'The Deserter', which each owe something to Owen's 'S.I.W.', as does his 'Ultima Ratio Regum' to Owen's 'Disabled'.

Rupert John Cornford was named after his mother's friend Rupert Brooke but when, unlike Auden and Spender, he went to fight in the Spanish Civil War (carrying the pistol his father had carried in the Great War), it was Owen who influenced his most famous poem, 'A Letter from Aragon'. In Owen's 'Dulce et Decorum Est' (see p. 27) the searing depiction of a gas attack is followed by an indignant direct address to the reader. Despite a disclaimer that 'There is no poison gas', Cornford's poem offers similar searing depictions of the battlefield and a similar direct address to the reader:

> But when I shook hands to leave, an Anarchist worker
> Said: 'Tell the workers of England
> This was a war not of our own making
> We did not seek it.
> But if ever the Fascists again rule Barcelona
> It will be as a heap of ruins with us workers beneath it.'

Cornford was dead but the Spanish Civil War still in progress when, in 1937, Yeats's *Oxford Book of Modern Verse* was published. No poem of Owen's was included and, in his Introduction, Yeats spent more time justifying his exclusion than the inclusion of most other poets:

> I have a distaste for certain poems written in the midst of the great war [....] The writers of these poems were invariably officers of exceptional courage and capacity, one a man constantly selected for dangerous work, all, I think, had the Military Cross; their letters are vivid and humorous, they were not without joy – for all skill is joyful – but felt bound, in the words of the best known, to plead the suffering of their men. In poems that had for a time considerable fame, written in the first person, they made that suffering their own. I have rejected these poems for the same reason that made Arnold withdraw his *Empedocles on Etna* from circulation; passive suffering is not theme for poetry.

Some of Yeats's inclusions – Grenfell's 'Into Battle', and seventeen poems by Oliver St John Gogarty (praised for his 'heroic song') – reveal his belief that the poet was one of the principal architects of civilization; his task, the representation of the great pagan images of love and war, passion and courage. The draft Preface to Owen's poems would, therefore, have seemed to him pernicious heresy, an abdication of the poet's traditional 'responsibility'. In the light of the furious debate prompted by Yeats's statement that 'passive suffering is not a theme for poetry', Owen's exclusion from the *Oxford Book* probably benefited – rather than harmed – his reputation.

It was Edmund Blunden, editor of the second edition of Owen's poems, who the following year introduced them to Keith Douglas, one of his undergraduates at Merton College, Oxford. That introduction was to play a part in shaping, arguably, the finest British poet of the Second World War. Temperamentally, Douglas was as unlike Owen as it was possible to be. The son of a decorated veteran of the Great

War, he had long had a romantic interest in warfare and, enlisting in a cavalry regiment in 1940, enscrolled a photograph of himself in uniform with the words '*Dulce et decorum est pro patria mori*'. Yeats would have approved of his *sprezzatura* and surely considered 'heroic song' Douglas's poem 'Gallantry', which begins:

The Colonel in a casual voice
spoke into the microphone a joke
which through a hundred earphones broke
into the ears of a doomed race.

Into the ears of the doomed boy, the fool
whose perfectly mannered flesh fell
in opening the door for a shell
as he had learnt to do at school.

One wonders what Owen – who wrote that his book was 'not about heroes' – would have made of this poem about 'three heroes'; its echo of his 'Doomed Youth'; its use of the pararhyme he pioneered (fool/fell); its thematic and linguistic links with his own poem 'The Last Laugh'. Douglas was not the first poet of the Second World War to echo Owen. On the other side of the Atlantic, Weldon Kees introduced his poem 'June 1940' with two epigraphs:

'*Yet these elegies are to this generation in no sense consolatory. They may be to the next. All a poet can do today is warn.*'

'*The old Lie: Dulce et Decorum est
Pro patria mori.*'

The voice of Wilfred Owen has continued to inspire his successors not only in time of war. Ted Hughes grew up in a Yorkshire household darkened by his father's memories of the First World War. In the 1950s, he wrote 'Wilfred Owen's Photographs', but a closer engagement with Owen emerges in one of his posthumous *Birthday Letters*, 'A Picture of Otto'. At a 'Strange Meeting' in hell (or hell on earth) with the ghost of Otto Plath, his wife Sylvia's father, Hughes echoes Owen's Preface ('if the spirit of [this book] survives – survives Prussia') when he says:

A big shock for so much of your Prussian backbone
As can be conjured into poetry
To find yourself so tangled with me –
Rising from your coffin, a big shock

To meet me face to face in the dark adit [....]

As in Owen's 'Strange Meeting', friend and enemy are conflated:

This underworld, my friend, is her heart's home.
Inseparable, here we must remain,

Everything forgiven and in common –
Not that I see her behind you, where I face you,
But like Owen, after his dark poem,
Under the battle, in the catacomb,

Sleeping with his German as if alone.

So much for the published evidence of the imaginative impact of Owen, the 'poet's poet', on the work of his successors. Its subconscious or subterranean impact is harder to determine, but Seamus Heaney gives us a rare glimpse of it in his lecture, 'Sixth Sense, Seventh Heaven':

By the time I wrote 'Bogland', I had been lecturing for a couple of years in Queen's University, and spoke every week to the students in First Arts English on the subject of modern poetry. One of the set books I most enjoyed teaching was Wilfred Owen's *Collected Poems* and one of the Owen poems I liked to focus on was 'Miners', which I myself had first encountered as a sixth former. It had come up as an unseen poem, an exercise in 'critical analysis and appreciation', and it made an unforgettable impression on me. Many things come together in it. The poet's comfort by a coal fire, for example, leads him to remember all those who, like coalminers and front-line soldiers, toil comfortlessly at the bottom of the social pyramid, carry its weight, are exploited by it, crushed by it, but still suffer in silence and retain their dignity. What makes the poem a real imaginative feat is the fact that Owen's moral indignation doesn't peel away from his sensuous language: the poet in him and the protester feel their way down the same intuitive paths, and while the burning coal shifts in the grate, these paths lead from a domestic interior to a geological and evolutionary panorama where all things are in a state of vegetal, even arcadian, bliss [....]

Harold Bloom's phrase 'the anxiety of influence', has had a great airing in the past couple of decades, but it is probably not the right way to describe how a poet feels about his or her susceptibility to another earlier poet's work. For example, when I remembered in the course of preparing this lecture that Owen's poem had been in my mind when I wrote 'Bogland', what I felt was closer to gratitude than anxiety. 'Miners' wasn't being imitated by me, but 'Bogland' was affected by the way 'Miners' shifted itself forward, its combination of free association and internal logic, its floating levels of earth and time. The movement and method of Owen's poem worked like a moving stair under my own, and are likely to have been more important than the archaeological data and bits of local boglore that made up much of the content.

Why have so many poets – not to mention so many general readers – responded so deeply to the work of a poet who, dying at twenty-five, saw only five of his poems in print and left many others to be re/constructed from manuscript by his editors? At the most superficial level, there is the romance of an early death that has come to seem emblematic of all the tragedies of the Great War. Young poets are often (in T. S.

Eliot's phrase) 'much possessed by death'. I was myself, but never read Owen's poems with any care until I was in my thirties and came to them by a curiously circuitous route. I was then 'much possessed' by Yeats and, invited to write an essay for a volume to be published in 1965 (his centenary year), chose as my topic 'Yeats as Anthologist'. Reconstructing the stormy history of his *Oxford Book of Modern Verse* (1936), I encountered the problem of why he omitted – and so disapproved of – Owen's work. The answer to this question quickened my interest in the younger poet.

Although Owen's Preface insists that his book 'is not about heroes', there is also the manifest heroism of a reluctant and vulnerable young officer, who led his 'boys' as well as a leader can and spoke of their sufferings as well as a pleader can. The power of his pleading challenges the validity of Yeats's pontifical dictum that 'passive suffering is not a theme for poetry'. Milton's sonnet on his blindness and many elegies speak of passive suffering, but are unquestionably poetry of the highest order. Moreover, as in the case of Milton's sonnet and elegies that similarly offer consolation, Owen's poems tend to make an active response to the suffering of which they speak. He is a classic example of what would become a quintessentially twentieth-century figure: the poet as witness – and not a passive witness. Most of his later and greater poems are fuelled by indignation. Introduced by Sassoon to the genre of the 'protest poem', he soon outgrew the two-dimensional poster-poem (such as 'The Dead-Beat') and tapped deeper and richer imaginative levels than ever Sassoon would reach.

The subject of his protest is often indicated by a title which the poem will subvert – 'The Parable of the Old Man and the Young', 'Smile, Smile, Smile', and 'Dulce et Decorum Est'. A similar strategy appears in his subversion of the literary epigraphs chosen for 'The Show', 'S.I.W.', and 'The Next War'; and the indignant response to other texts that kick-start 'Anthem for Doomed Youth', the fragment 'Cramped in that funnelled hole' and 'Dulce et Decorum Est' (see the notes to these three poems on page 65–6).

Owen's readiness to express his feelings – of grief, tenderness, delight, as well as indignation – is a significant part of his appeal. Readers are often moved by the immediacy of his work before they appreciate the subtle density of its literary allusion. So with its music. In February 1918, he told Leslie Gunston: 'I suppose I am doing in poetry what the advanced composers are doing in music.' Apprenticed to Keats and Shelley, he had absorbed the traditions of harmony and rhetoric they inherited and extended. The harmonic tradition he himself extended with his pioneering use of 'pararhymes': escaped/scooped, groined/groaned. In 'Strange Meeting' (p. 32), from which these examples are taken, the second rhyme is usually lower in pitch than the first, giving the couplet 'a dying fall' that musically reinforces the poem's meaning; the tragedy of the German poet (one manuscript reads 'I was a German conscript, and your friend'), his life cut short by the British poet whom he meets in Hell. In the poem 'Miners' (p. 22), the pitch of the pararhymes rises and falls as the sense moves from grief to happiness and back to grief again:

> The centuries will burn rich loads
>   With which we groaned,
> Whose warmth shall lull their dreaming lids,
>   While songs are crooned;
> But they will not dream of us poor lads,
>   Left in the ground.

The same poem offers an example of another of Owen's harmonic innovations – the punning internal rhyme of 'wry [....] writhing', found also in the 'Men [....] Many' of 'Dulce and Decorum Est'.

What finally sets him apart from all but his most major contemporaries, however, is a breadth and depth of vision that in 'Futility', for example, can hold – as it were in the palm of a hand – the grand and the granular together:

Move him into the sun –
Gently its touch awoke him once,
At home, whispering of fields half-sown.
Always it woke him, even in France,
Until this morning and this snow.
If anything might rouse him now
The kind old sun will know.

Think how it wakes the seeds –
Woke once the clays of a cold star.
Are limbs, so dear achieved, are sides
Full-nerved, still warm, too hard to stir?
Was it for this the clay grew tall?
– O what made fatuous sunbeams toil
To break earth's sleep at all?

So, in the larger meditative structure of 'Insensibility', Owen
can move with no loss of tension from the colloquial to the
cosmic, from 'poets' tearful fooling' to 'the eternal reciprocity
of tears', a phrase that even Shakespeare might have envied.

JON STALLWORTHY

WILFRED OWEN

Sonnet

Written at Teignmouth, on a Pilgrimage to Keats's House

Three colours have I known the Deep to wear;
'Tis well today that Purple grandeurs gloom,
Veiling the Emerald sheen and Sky-blue glare.
Well, too, that lowly-brooding clouds now loom
In sable majesty around, fringed fair
With ermine-white of surf: to me they bear
Watery memorials of His mystic doom
Whose Name was writ in Water (saith his tomb).

Eternally may sad waves wail his death,
Choke in their grief 'mongst rocks where he has lain,
Or heave in silence, yearning with hushed breath,
While mournfully trail the slow-moved mists and rain,
And softly the small drops slide from weeping trees,
Quivering in anguish to the sobbing breeze.

Uriconium

An Ode

It lieth low near merry England's heart
Like a long-buried sin; and Englishmen
Forget that in its death their sires had part.
And, like a sin, Time lays it bare again

    To tell of races wronged,
And ancient glories suddenly overcast,
And treasures flung to fire and rabble wrath.

    If thou hast ever longed
To lift the gloomy curtain of Time Past,
And spy the secret things that Hades hath,
Here through this riven ground take such a view.
The dust, that fell unnoted as a dew,
Wrapped the dead city's face like mummy-cloth:
All is as was: except for worm and moth.

Since Jove was worshipped under Wrekin's shade
Or Latin phrase was writ in Shropshire stone,
Since Druid chaunts desponded in this glade
Or Tuscan general called that field his own,

    How long ago? How long?
How long since wanderers in the Stretton Hills
Met men of shaggy hair and savage jaw,

    With flint and copper prong,
Aiming behind their dikes and thorny grilles?

    Ah! those were days before the axe and saw,
    Then were the nights when this mid-forest town
    Held breath to hear the wolves come yelping down,
    And ponderous bears 'long Severn lifted paw,
    And nuzzling boars ran grunting through the shaw.

Ah me! full fifteen hundred times the wheat
Hath risen, and bowed, and fallen to human hunger
Since those imperial days were made complete.

4

The weary moon hath waxen old and younger
　　These eighteen thousand times
Without a shrine to greet her gentle ray.
And other temples rose; to Power and Pelf,
　　And chimed centurial chimes
Until their very bells are worn away.
While King by King lay cold on vaulted shelf
And wars closed wars, and many a Marmion fell,
And dearths and plagues holp sire and son to hell;
And old age stiffened many a lively elf
And many a poet's heart outdrained itself.

I had forgot that so remote an age
Beyond the horizon of our little sight,
Is far from us by no more spanless gauge
Than day and night, succeeding day and night,
　　Until I looked on Thee,
Thou ghost of a dead city, or its husk!
But even as we could walk by field and hedge
　　Hence to the distant sea
So, by the rote of common dawn and dusk,
We travel back to history's utmost edge.
Yea, when through thy old streets I took my way,
And recked a thousand years as yesterday,
Methought sage fancy wrought a sacrilege
To steal for me such godly privilege!

For here lie remnants from a banquet table –
Oysters and marrow-bones, and seeds of grape –
The statement of whose age must sound a fable;
And Samian jars, whose sheen and flawless shape
　　Look fresh from potter's mould.
Plasters with Roman finger-marks impressed;
Bracelets, that from the warm Italian arm
　　Might seem to be scarce cold;
And spears – the same that pushed the Cymry west –
Unblunted yet; with tools of forge and farm

Abandoned, as a man in sudden fear
Drops what he holds to help his swift career:
For sudden was Rome's flight, and wild the alarm.
The Saxon shock was like Vesuvius' qualm.

O ye who prate of modern art and craft
Mark well that Gaulish brooch, and test that screw!
Art's fairest buds on antique stem are graft.
Under the sun is nothing wholly new!
    At Viricon today
The village anvil rests on Roman base
And in a garden, may be seen a bower
    With pillars for its stay
That anciently in basilic had place.
The church's font is but a pagan dower:
A Temple's column, hollowed into this.
So is the glory of our artifice,
Our pleasure and our worship, but the flower
Of Roman custom and of Roman power.

O ye who laugh and, living as if Time
Meant but the twelve hours ticking round your dial,
Find it too short for thee, watch the sublime,
Slow, epochal time-registers awhile,
    Which are Antiquities.
O ye who weep and call all your life too long
And moan: Was ever sorrow like to mine?
    Muse on the memories
That sad sepulchral stones and ruins prolong.
Here might men drink of wonder like strong wine
And feel ephemeral troubles soothed and curbed.
Yet farmers, wroth to have their laws disturbed,
Are sooner roused for little loss to pine
Than we are moved by mighty woes long syne.

Above this reverend ground, what traveller checks?
Yet cities such as these one time would breed

Apocalyptic visions of world-wrecks.
Let Saxon men return to them, and heed!
  They slew and burnt,
But after, prized what Rome had given away
Out of her strength and her prosperity.
  Have they yet learnt
The precious truth distilled from Rome's decay?
Ruins! On England's heart press heavily!
For Rome hath left us more than walls and words
And better yet shall leave; and more than herds
Or land or gold gave the Celts to us in fee;
E'en Blood, which makes poets sing and prophets see.

Long Ages Past

Long ages past in Egypt thou wert worshipped
And thou wert wrought from ivory and beryl.
They brought thee jewels and they brought their slain,
Thy feet were dark with blood of sacrifice.
From dawn to midnight, O my painted idol,
Thou satest smiling, and the noise of killing
Was harp and timbrel in thy pale jade ears;
The livid dead were given thee for toys.

Thou wert a mad slave in a Persian palace,
And the King loved thee for thy furious beauty,
And all men heard thy ravings with a smile
Because thy face was fairer than a flower.
But with a little knife so wantonly
Thou slewest women and thy pining lovers,
And on thy lips the stain of crimson blood,
And on thy brow the pallor of their death.

Thou art the dream beheld by frenzied princes
In smoke of opium. Thou art the last fulfilment
Of all the wicked, and of all the beautiful.
We hold thee as a poppy to our mouths,
Finding with thee forgetfulness of God.
Thou art the face reflected in a mirror
Of wild desire, of pain, of bitter pleasure.
The witches shout thy name beneath the moon,
The fires of Hell have held thee in their fangs.

'O World of many worlds'

O World of many worlds, O life of lives,
    What centre hast thou? Where am I?
O whither is it thy fierce onrush drives?
    Fight I, or drift; or stand; or fly?

The loud machinery spins, points work in touch;
    Wheels whirl in systems, zone in zone.
Myself, having sometime moved with such,
    Would strike a centre of mine own.

Lend hand, O Fate, for I am down, am lost!
    Fainting by violence of the Dance ...
Ah thanks, I stand – the floor is crossed,
    And I am where but few advance.

I see men far below me where they swarm ...
    (Haply *above* me – be it so!
Does space to compass-points conform,
    And can we say a star stands high or low?)

Not more complex the millions of the stars
    Than are the hearts of mortal brothers;
As far remote as Neptune from small Mars
    Is one man's nature from another's.

But all hold course unalterably fixed;
    They follow destinies foreplanned:
I envy not these lives their faith unmixed,
    I would not step with such a band.

To be a meteor, fast, eccentric, lone,
    Lawless; in passage through all spheres,
Warning the earth of wider ways unknown
    And rousing men with heavenly fears ...

This is the track reserved for my endeavour;
   Spanless the erring way I wend.
Blackness of darkness is my meed for ever?
   And barren plunging without end?

O glorious fear! Those other wandering souls
   High burning through that outer bourne
Are lights unto themselves. Fair aureoles
   Self-radiated there are worn.

And when in after times those stars return
   And strike once more earth's horizon,
They gather many satellites astern,
   For they are greater than this system's Sun.

Inspection

'You! What d'you mean by this?' I rapped.
'You dare come on parade like this?'
'Please, sir, it's – ' ''Old yer mouth,' the sergeant snapped.
'I takes 'is name, sir?' – 'Please, and then dismiss.'

Some days 'confined to camp' he got,
For being 'dirty on parade'.
He told me, afterwards, the damnèd spot
Was blood, his own. 'Well, blood is dirt,' I said.

'Blood's dirt,' he laughed, looking away,
Far off to where his wound had bled
And almost merged for ever into clay.
'The world is washing out its stains,' he said.
'It doesn't like our cheeks so red:
Young blood's its great objection.
But when we're duly white-washed, being dead,
The race will bear Field Marshal God's inspection.'

With an Identity Disc

If ever I had dreamed of my dead name
High in the heart of London, unsurpassed
By Time for ever, and the Fugitive, Fame,
There taking a long sanctuary at last,

I better that; and recollect with shame
How once I longed to hide it from life's heats
Under those holy cypresses, the same
That keep in shade the quiet place of Keats.

Now, rather, thank I God there is no risk
Of gravers scoring it with florid screed,
But let my death be memoried on this disc.
Wear it, sweet friend. Inscribe no date nor deed.
But let thy heart-beat kiss it night and day,
Until the name grow vague and wear away.

Anthem for Doomed Youth

What passing-bells for these who die as cattle?
   – Only the monstrous anger of the guns.
   Only the stuttering rifles' rapid rattle
Can patter out their hasty orisons.
No mockeries now for them; no prayers nor bells;
   Nor any voice of mourning save the choirs, –
The shrill, demented choirs of wailing shells;
   And bugles calling for them from sad shires.

What candles may be held to speed them all?
   Not in the hands of boys but in their eyes
Shall shine the holy glimmers of goodbyes.
   The pallor of girls' brows shall be their pall;
Their flowers the tenderness of patient minds,
And each slow dusk a drawing-down of blinds.

1914

War broke: and now the Winter of the world
With perishing great darkness closes in.
The foul tornado, centred at Berlin,
Is over all the width of Europe whirled,
Rending the sails of progress. Rent or furled
Are all Art's ensigns. Verse wails. Now begin
Famines of thought and feeling. Love's wine's thin.
The grain of human Autumn rots, down-hurled.

For after Spring had bloomed in early Greece,
And Summer blazed her glory out with Rome,
An Autumn softly fell, a harvest home,
A slow grand age, and rich with all increase.
But now, for us, wild Winter, and the need
Of sowings for new Spring, and blood for seed.

From My Diary, July 1914

Leaves
  Murmuring by myriads in the shimmering trees.
Lives
  Wakening with wonder in the Pyrenees.
Birds
  Cheerily chirping in the early day.
Bards
  Singing of summer, scything through the hay.
Bees
  Shaking the heavy dews from bloom and frond.
Boys
  Bursting the surface of the ebony pond.
Flashes
  Of swimmers carving through the sparkling cold.
Fleshes
  Gleaming with wetness to the morning gold.
A mead
  Bordered about with warbling waterbrooks.
A maid
  Laughing the love-laugh with me; proud of looks.
The heat
  Throbbing between the upland and the peak.
Her heart
  Quivering with passion to my pressèd cheek.
Braiding
  Of floating flames across the mountain brow.
Brooding
  Of stillness; and a sighing of the bough.
Stirs
  Of leaflets in the gloom; soft petal-showers;
Stars
  Expanding with the starr'd nocturnal flowers.

Apologia pro Poemate Meo

I, too, saw God through mud, –
    The mud that cracked on cheeks when wretches smiled.
    War brought more glory to their eyes than blood,
    And gave their laughs more glee than shakes a child.

Merry it was to laugh there –
    Where death becomes absurd and life absurder.
    For power was on us as we slashed bones bare
    Not to feel sickness or remorse of murder.

I, too, have dropped off Fear –
    Behind the barrage, dead as my platoon,
    And sailed my spirit surging light and clear
    Past the entanglement where hopes lay strewn;

And witnessed exultation –
    Faces that used to curse me, scowl for scowl,
    Shine and lift up with passion of oblation,
    Seraphic for an hour; though they were foul.

I have made fellowships –
    Untold of happy lovers in old song.
    For love is not the binding of fair lips
    With the soft silk of eyes that look and long,

By Joy, whose ribbon slips, –
    But wound with war's hard wire whose stakes are strong;
    Bound with the bandage of the arm that drips;
    Knit in the webbing of the rifle-thong.

I have perceived much beauty
    In the hoarse oaths that kept our courage straight;
    Heard music in the silentness of duty;
    Found peace where shell-storms spouted reddest spate.

Nevertheless, except you share
　　With them in hell the sorrowful dark of hell,
　　Whose world is but the trembling of a flare
　　And heaven but as the highway for a shell,

You shall not hear their mirth:
　　You shall not come to think them well content
　　By any jest of mine. These men are worth
　　Your tears. You are not worth their merriment.

Le Christianisme

So the church Christ was hit and buried
  Under its rubbish and its rubble.
In cellars, packed-up saints lie serried,
  Well out of hearing of our trouble.

One Virgin still immaculate
  Smiles on for war to flatter her.
She's halo'd with an old tin hat,
  But a piece of hell will batter her.

'Cramped in that funnelled hole'

Cramped in that funnelled hole, they watched the dawn
Open a jagged rim around; a yawn
Of death's jaws, which had all but swallowed them
Stuck in the bottom of his throat of phlegm.

They were in one of many mouths of Hell
Not seen of seers in visions; only felt
As teeth of traps; when bones and the dead are smelt
Under the mud where long ago they fell
Mixed with the sour sharp odour of the shell.

Hospital Barge

Budging the sluggard ripples of the Somme,
A barge round old Cérisy slowly slewed.
Softly her engines down the current screwed,
And chuckled softly with contented hum,
Till fairy tinklings struck their croonings dumb.
The waters rumpling at the stern subdued;
The lock-gate took her bulging amplitude;
Gently from out the gurgling lock she swum.

One reading by that calm bank shaded eyes
To watch her lessening westward quietly.
Then, as she neared the bend, her funnel screamed.
And that long lamentation made him wise
How unto Avalon, in agony,
Kings passed in the dark barge which Merlin dreamed.

At a Calvary near the Ancre

One ever hangs where shelled roads part.
   In this war He too lost a limb,
But His disciples hide apart;
   And now the Soldiers bear with Him.

Near Golgotha strolls many a priest,
   And in their faces there is pride
That they were flesh-marked by the Beast
   By whom the gentle Christ's denied.

The scribes on all the people shove
   And bawl allegiance to the state,
But they who love the greater love
   Lay down their life; they do not hate.

Miners

There was a whispering in my hearth,
    A sigh of the coal,
Grown wistful of a former earth
    It might recall.

I listened for a tale of leaves
    And smothered ferns,
Frond-forests, and the low sly lives
    Before the fauns.

My fire might show steam-phantoms simmer
    From Time's old cauldron,
Before the birds made nests in summer,
    Or men had children.

But the coals were murmuring of their mine,
    And moans down there
Of boys that slept wry sleep, and men
    Writhing for air.

And I saw white bones in the cinder-shard,
    Bones without number.
Many the muscled bodies charred,
    And few remember.

I thought of all that worked dark pits
    Of war, and died
Digging the rock where Death reputes
    Peace lies indeed.

Comforted years will sit soft-chaired,
    In rooms of amber;
The years will stretch their hands, well-cheered
    By our life's ember;

The centuries will burn rich loads
    With which we groaned,
Whose warmth shall lull their dreaming lids,
    While songs are crooned;
But they will not dream of us poor lads,
    Left in the ground.

The Letter

With B.E.F. June 10. Dear Wife,
(Oh blast this pencil. 'Ere, Bill, lend's a knife.)
I'm in the pink at present, dear.
I think the war will end this year.
We don't see much of them square-'eaded 'Uns.
We're out of harm's way, not bad fed.
I'm longing for a taste of your old buns.
(Say, Jimmie, spare's a bite of bread.)
There don't seem much to say just now.
(Yer what? Then don't, yer ruddy cow!
And give us back me cigarette!)
I'll soon be 'ome. You mustn't fret.
My feet's improvin', as I told you of.
We're out in rest now. Never fear.
(VRACH! By crumbs, but that was near.)
Mother might spare you half a sov.
Kiss Nell and Bert. When me and you –
(Eh? What the 'ell! Stand to? Stand to!
Jim, give's a hand with pack on, lad.
Guh! Christ! I'm hit. Take 'old. Aye, bad.
No, damn your iodine. Jim? 'Ere!
Write my old girl, Jim, there's a dear.)

Conscious

His fingers wake, and flutter; up the bed.
His eyes come open with a pull of will,
Helped by the yellow mayflowers by his head.
The blind-cord drawls across the window-sill ...
What a smooth floor the ward has! What a rug!
Who is that talking somewhere out of sight?
Three flies are creeping round the shiny jug ...
'Nurse! Doctor!' – 'Yes, all right, all right.'

But sudden evening blurs and fogs the air.
There seems no time to want a drink of water.
Nurse looks so far away. And here and there
Music and roses burst through crimson slaughter.
He can't remember where he saw blue sky ...
The trench is narrower. Cold, he's cold; yet hot –
And there's no light to see the voices by ...
There is no time to ask ... he knows not what.

Schoolmistress

Having, with bold Horatius, stamped her feet
And waved a final swashing arabesque
O'er the brave days of old, she ceased to bleat,
Slapped her Macaulay back upon the desk,
Resumed her calm gaze and her lofty seat.

There, while she heard the classic lines repeat,
Once more the teacher's face clenched stern;
For through the window, looking on the street,
Three soldiers hailed her. She made no return.
One was called 'Orace whom she would not greet.

Dulce et Decorum Est

Bent double, like old beggars under sacks,
Knock-kneed, coughing like hags, we cursed through sludge,
Till on the haunting flares we turned our backs
And towards our distant rest began to trudge.
Men marched asleep. Many had lost their boots
But limped on, blood-shod. All went lame; all blind;
Drunk with fatigue; deaf even to the hoots
Of tired, outstripped Five-Nines that dropped behind.

Gas! GAS! Quick, boys! – An ecstasy of fumbling,
Fitting the clumsy helmets just in time;
But someone still was yelling out and stumbling,
And flound'ring like a man in fire or lime ...
Dim, through the misty panes and thick green light,
As under a green sea, I saw him drowning.

In all my dreams, before my helpless sight,
He plunges at me, guttering, choking, drowning.

If in some smothering dreams you too could pace
Behind the wagon that we flung him in,
And watch the white eyes writhing in his face,
His hanging face, like a devil's sick of sin;
If you could hear, at every jolt, the blood
Come gargling from the froth-corrupted lungs,
Obscene as cancer, bitter as the cud
Of vile, incurable sores on innocent tongues, –
My friend, you would not tell with such high zest
To children ardent for some desperate glory,
The old Lie: Dulce et decorum est
Pro patria mori.

The Dead-Beat

He dropped, – more sullenly than wearily,
Lay stupid like a cod, heavy like meat,
And none of us could kick him to his feet;
– Just blinked at my revolver, blearily;
– Didn't appear to know a war was on,
Or see the blasted trench at which he stared.
'I'll do 'em in,' he whined. 'If this hand's spared,
I'll murder them, I will.'

                 A low voice said,
'It's Blighty, p'raps, he sees; his pluck's all gone,
Dreaming of all the valiant, that *aren't* dead:
Bold uncles, smiling ministerially;
Maybe his brave young wife, getting her fun
In some new home, improved materially.
It's not these stiffs have crazed him; nor the Hun.'

We sent him down at last, out of the way.
Unwounded; – stout lad, too, before that strafe.
Malingering? Stretcher-bearers winked, 'Not half!'

Next day I heard the Doc's well-whiskied laugh:
'That scum you sent last night soon died. Hooray!'

Insensibility

1

Happy are men who yet before they are killed
Can let their veins run cold.
Whom no compassion fleers
Or makes their feet
Sore on the alleys cobbled with their brothers.
The front line withers.
But they are troops who fade, not flowers,
For poets' tearful fooling:
Men, gaps for filling:
Losses, who might have fought
Longer; but no one bothers.

2

And some cease feeling
Even themselves or for themselves.
Dullness best solves
The tease and doubt of shelling,
And Chance's strange arithmetic
Comes simpler than the reckoning of their shilling.
They keep no check on armies' decimation.

3

Happy are these who lose imagination:
They have enough to carry with ammunition.
Their spirit drags no pack.
Their old wounds, save with cold, can not more ache.
Having seen all things red,
Their eyes are rid
Of the hurt of the colour of blood for ever.
And terror's first constriction over,

Their hearts remain small-drawn.
Their senses in some scorching cautery of battle
Now long since ironed,
Can laugh among the dying, unconcerned.

4

Happy the soldier home, with not a notion
How somewhere, every dawn, some men attack,
And many sighs are drained.
Happy the lad whose mind was never trained:
His days are worth forgetting more than not.
He sings along the march
Which we march taciturn, because of dusk,
The long, forlorn, relentless trend
From larger day to huger night.

5

We wise, who with a thought besmirch
Blood over all our soul,
How should we see our task
But through his blunt and lashless eyes?
Alive, he is not vital overmuch;
Dying, not mortal overmuch;
Nor sad, nor proud,
Nor curious at all.
He cannot tell
Old men's placidity from his.

6

But cursed are dullards whom no cannon stuns,
That they should be as stones.
Wretched are they, and mean
With paucity that never was simplicity.
By choice they made themselves immune

To pity and whatever moans in man
Before the last sea and the hapless stars;
Whatever mourns when many leave these shores;
Whatever shares
The eternal reciprocity of tears.

Strange Meeting

It seemed that out of battle I escaped
Down some profound dull tunnel, long since scooped
Through granites which titanic wars had groined.

Yet also there encumbered sleepers groaned,
Too fast in thought or death to be bestirred.
Then, as I probed them, one sprang up, and stared
With piteous recognition in fixed eyes,
Lifting distressful hands, as if to bless.
And by his smile, I knew that sullen hall, –
By his dead smile I knew we stood in Hell.

With a thousand pains that vision's face was grained;
Yet no blood reached there from the upper ground,
And no guns thumped, or down the flues made moan.
'Strange friend,' I said, 'here is no cause to mourn.'
'None,' said that other, 'save the undone years,
The hopelessness. Whatever hope is yours,
Was my life also; I went hunting wild
After the wildest beauty in the world,
Which lies not calm in eyes, or braided hair,
But mocks the steady running of the hour,
And if it grieves, grieves richlier than here.
For by my glee might many men have laughed,
And of my weeping something had been left,
Which must die now. I mean the truth untold,
The pity of war, the pity war distilled.
Now men will go content with what we spoiled,
Or, discontent, boil bloody, and be spilled.
They will be swift with swiftness of the tigress.
None will break ranks, though nations trek from progress.
Courage was mine, and I had mystery,
Wisdom was mine, and I had mastery:
To miss the march of this retreating world

Into vain citadels that are not walled.
Then, when much blood had clogged their chariot-wheels,
I would go up and wash them from sweet wells,
Even with truths that lie too deep for taint.
I would have poured my spirit without stint
But not through wounds; not on the cess of war.
Foreheads of men have bled where no wounds were.

'I am the enemy you killed, my friend.
I knew you in this dark: for so you frowned
Yesterday through me as you jabbed and killed.
I parried; but my hands were loath and cold.
Let us sleep now ...'

Sonnet

On Seeing a Piece of Our Heavy Artillery Brought into Action

Be slowly lifted up, thou long black arm,
Great Gun towering towards Heaven, about to curse;
Sway steep against them, and for years rehearse
Huge imprecations like a blasting charm!
Reach at that Arrogance which needs thy harm,
And beat it down before its sins grow worse.
Spend our resentment, cannon, – yea, disburse
Our gold in shapes of flame, our breaths in storm.

Yet, for men's sakes whom thy vast malison
Must wither innocent of enmity,
Be not withdrawn, dark arm, thy spoilure done,
Safe to the bosom of our prosperity.
But when thy spell be cast complete and whole,
May God curse thee, and cut thee from our soul!

Asleep

Under his helmet, up against his pack,
After so many days of work and waking,
Sleep took him by the brow and laid him back.

There, in the happy no-time of his sleeping,
Death took him by the heart. There heaved a quaking
Of the aborted life within him leaping,
Then chest and sleepy arms once more fell slack.

And soon the slow, stray blood came creeping
From the intruding lead, like ants on track.

Whether his deeper sleep lie shaded by the shaking
Of great wings, and the thoughts that hung the stars,
High-pillowed on calm pillows of God's making,
Above these clouds, these rains, these sleets of lead,
And these winds' scimitars,
– Or whether yet his thin and sodden head
Confuses more and more with the low mould,
His hair being one with the grey grass
Of finished fields, and wire-scrags rusty-old,
Who knows? Who hopes? Who troubles? Let it pass!
He sleeps. He sleeps less tremulous, less cold,
Than we who wake, and waking say Alas!

Arms and the Boy

Let the boy try along this bayonet-blade
How cold steel is, and keen with hunger of blood;
Blue with all malice, like a madman's flash;
And thinly drawn with famishing for flesh.

Lend him to stroke these blind, blunt bullet-leads,
Which long to nuzzle in the hearts of lads,
Or give him cartridges whose fine zinc teeth
Are sharp with sharpness of grief and death.

For his teeth seem for laughing round an apple.
There lurk no claws behind his fingers supple;
And God will grow no talons at his heels,
Nor antlers through the thickness of his curls.

The Show

We have fallen in the dreams the ever-living
Breathe on the tarnished mirror of the world,
And then smooth out with ivory hands and sigh.

W. B. YEATS

My soul looked down from a vague height, with Death,
As unremembering how I rose or why,
And saw a sad land, weak with sweats of dearth,
Grey, cratered like the moon with hollow woe,
And pitted with great pocks and scabs of plagues.

Across its beard, that horror of harsh wire,
There moved thin caterpillars, slowly uncoiled.
It seemed they pushed themselves to be as plugs
Of ditches, where they writhed and shrivelled, killed.

By them had slimy paths been trailed and scraped
Round myriad warts that might be little hills.

From gloom's last dregs these long-strung creatures crept,
And vanished out of dawn down hidden holes.

(And smell came up from those foul openings
As out of mouths, or deep wounds deepening.)

On dithering feet upgathered, more and more,
Brown strings, towards strings of grey, with bristling spines,
All migrants from green fields, intent on mire.

Those that were grey, of more abundant spawns,
Ramped on the rest and ate them and were eaten.

I saw their bitten backs curve, loop, and straighten.
I watched those agonies curl, lift, and flatten.

Whereat, in terror what that sight might mean,
I reeled and shivered earthward like a feather.

And Death fell with me, like a deepening moan.
And He, picking a manner of worm, which half had hid
Its bruises in the earth, but crawled no further,
Showed me its feet, the feet of many men,
And the fresh-severed head of it, my head.

Futility

Move him into the sun –
Gently its touch awoke him once,
At home, whispering of fields half-sown.
Always it woke him, even in France,
Until this morning and this snow.
If anything might rouse him now
The kind old sun will know.

Think how it wakes the seeds –
Woke once the clays of a cold star.
Are limbs, so dear achieved, are sides
Full-nerved, still warm, too hard to stir?
Was it for this the clay grew tall?
– O what made fatuous sunbeams toil
To break earth's sleep at all?

The End

After the blast of lightning from the east,
  The flourish of loud clouds, the Chariot Throne;
After the drums of time have rolled and ceased,
  And by the bronze west long retreat is blown,
Shall Life renew these bodies? Of a truth,
  All death will he annul, all tears assuage?
Or fill these void veins full again with youth,
  And wash, with an immortal water, age?

When I do ask white Age, he saith not so:
  'My head hangs weighed with snow.'
And when I hearken to the Earth, she saith:
  'My fiery heart shrinks, aching. It is death.
Mine ancient scars shall not be glorified,
Nor my titanic tears, the seas, be dried.'

S.I.W.

I will to the King,
And offer him consolation in his trouble,
For that man there has set his teeth to die,
And being one that hates obedience,
Discipline, and orderliness of life,
I cannot mourn him.

W. B. YEATS

1   The Prologue

Patting goodbye, doubtless they told the lad
He'd always show the Hun a brave man's face;
Father would sooner him dead than in disgrace, –
Was proud to see him going, aye, and glad.
Perhaps his mother whimpered how she'd fret
Until he got a nice safe wound to nurse.
Sisters would wish girls too could shoot, charge, curse . . .
Brothers – would send his favourite cigarette.
Each week, month after month, they wrote the same,
Thinking him sheltered in some Y. M. Hut,
Because he said so, writing on his butt
Where once an hour a bullet missed its aim.
And misses teased the hunger of his brain.
His eyes grew old with wincing, and his hand
Reckless with ague. Courage leaked, as sand
From the best sandbags after years of rain.
But never leave, wound, fever, trench-foot, shock,
Untrapped the wretch. And death seemed still withheld
For torture of lying machinally shelled,
At the pleasure of this world's Powers who'd run amok.

He'd seen men shoot their hands, on night patrol.
Their people never knew. Yet they were vile.
'Death sooner than dishonour, that's the style!'
So Father said.

II The Action

                    One dawn, our wire patrol
Carried him. This time, Death had not missed.
We could do nothing but wipe his bleeding cough.
Could it be accident? – Rifles go off . . .
Not sniped? No. (Later they found the English ball.)

III The Poem

It was the reasoned crisis of his soul
Against more days of inescapable thrall,
Against infrangibly wired and blind trench wall
Curtained with fire, roofed in with creeping fire,
Slow grazing fire, that would not burn him whole
But kept him for death's promises and scoff,
And life's half-promising, and both their riling.

IV The Epilogue

With him they buried the muzzle his teeth had kissed,
And truthfully wrote the mother, 'Tim died smiling.'

The Next War

War's a joke for me and you,
While we know such dreams are true.

SIEGFRIED SASSOON

Out there, we walked quite friendly up to Death, –
   Sat down and ate beside him, cool and bland, –
   Pardoned his spilling mess-tins in our hand.
We've sniffed the green thick odour of his breath, –
Our eyes wept, but our courage didn't writhe.
   He's spat at us with bullets, and he's coughed
   Shrapnel. We chorused if he sang aloft,
We whistled while he shaved us with his scythe.

Oh, Death was never enemy of ours!
   We laughed at him, we leagued with him, old chum.
No soldier's paid to kick against His powers.
   We laughed, – knowing that better men would come,
And greater wars: when every fighter brags
He fights on Death, for lives; not men, for flags.

Greater Love

Red lips are not so red
  As the stained stones kissed by the English dead.
Kindness of wooed and wooer
Seems shame to their love pure.
O Love, your eyes lose lure
  When I behold eyes blinded in my stead!

Your slender attitude
  Trembles not exquisite like limbs knife-skewed,
Rolling and rolling there
Where God seems not to care;
Till the fierce love they bear
  Cramps them in death's extreme decrepitude.

Your voice sings not so soft, –
  Though even as wind murmuring through raftered loft, –
Your dear voice is not dear,
Gentle, and evening clear,
As theirs whom none now hear,
  Now earth has stopped their piteous mouths that coughed.

Heart, you were never hot
  Nor large, nor full like hearts made great with shot;
And though your hand be pale,
Paler are all which trail
Your cross through flame and hail:
  Weep, you may weep, for you may touch them not.

The Last Laugh

'Oh! Jesus Christ! I'm hit,' he said; and died.
Whether he vainly cursed or prayed indeed,
      The Bullets chirped – In vain, vain, vain!
      Machine-guns chuckled – Tut-tut! Tut-tut!
      And the Big Gun guffawed.

Another sighed – 'O Mother, – Mother, – Dad!'
Then smiled at nothing, childlike, being dead.
      And the lofty Shrapnel-cloud
      Leisurely gestured, – Fool!
      And the splinters spat, and tittered.

'My Love!' one moaned. Love-languid seemed his mood,
Till slowly lowered, his whole face kissed the mud.
      And the Bayonets' long teeth grinned;
      Rabbles of Shells hooted and groaned;
      And the Gas hissed.

Mental Cases

Who are these? Why sit they here in twilight?
Wherefore rock they, purgatorial shadows,
Drooping tongues from jaws that slob their relish,
Baring teeth that leer like skulls' teeth wicked?
Stroke on stroke of pain,– but what slow panic,
Gouged these chasms round their fretted sockets?
Ever from their hair and through their hands' palms
Misery swelters. Surely we have perished
Sleeping, and walk hell; but who these hellish?

– These are men whose minds the Dead have ravished.
Memory fingers in their hair of murders,
Multitudinous murders they once witnessed.
Wading sloughs of flesh these helpless wander,
Treading blood from lungs that had loved laughter.
Always they must see these things and hear them,
Batter of guns and shatter of flying muscles,
Carnage incomparable, and human squander
Rucked too thick for these men's extrication.

Therefore still their eyeballs shrink tormented
Back into their brains, because on their sense
Sunlight seems a blood-smear; night comes blood-black;
Dawn breaks open like a wound that bleeds afresh.
– Thus their heads wear this hilarious, hideous,
Awful falseness of set-smiling corpses.
– Thus their hands are plucking at each other;
Picking at the rope-knouts of their scourging;
Snatching after us who smote them, brother,
Pawing us who dealt them war and madness.

The Chances

I 'mind as how the night before that show
Us five got talkin'; we was in the know.
'Ah well,' says Jimmy, and he's seen some scrappin',
'There ain't no more than five things as can happen, –
You get knocked out; else wounded, bad or cushy;
Scuppered; or nowt except you're feelin' mushy.'

One of us got the knock-out, blown to chops;
One lad was hurt, like, losin' both his props;
And one – to use the word of hypocrites –
Had the misfortune to be took by Fritz.
Now me, I wasn't scratched, praise God Almighty,
Though next time please I'll thank Him for a blighty.
But poor old Jim, he's livin' and he's not;
He reckoned he'd five chances, and he had:
He's wounded, killed, and pris'ner, all the lot,
The flamin' lot all rolled in one. Jim's mad.

The Send-off

Down the close darkening lanes they sang their way
To the siding-shed,
And lined the train with faces grimly gay.

Their breasts were stuck all white with wreath and spray
As men's are, dead.

Dull porters watched them, and a casual tramp
Stood staring hard,
Sorry to miss them from the upland camp.

Then, unmoved, signals nodded, and a lamp
Winked to the guard.

So secretly, like wrongs hushed-up, they went.
They were not ours:
We never heard to which front these were sent;

Nor there if they yet mock what women meant
Who gave them flowers.

Shall they return to beating of great bells
In wild train-loads?
A few, a few, too few for drums and yells,

May creep back, silent, to village wells,
Up half-known roads.

The Parable of the Old Man and the Young

So Abram rose, and clave the wood, and went,
And took the fire with him, and a knife.
And as they sojourned both of them together,
Isaac the first-born spake and said, My Father,
Behold the preparations, fire and iron,
But where the lamb, for this burnt-offering?
Then Abram bound the youth with belts and straps,
And builded parapets and trenches there,
And stretchèd forth the knife to slay his son.
When lo! an Angel called him out of heaven,
Saying, Lay not thy hand upon the lad,
Neither do anything to him, thy son.
Behold! Caught in a thicket by its horns,
A Ram. Offer the Ram of Pride instead.

But the old man would not so, but slew his son,
And half the seed of Europe, one by one.

Disabled

He sat in a wheeled chair, waiting for dark,
And shivered in his ghastly suit of grey,
Legless, sewn short at elbow. Through the park
Voices of boys rang saddening like a hymn,
Voices of play and pleasure after day,
Till gathering sleep had mothered them from him.

*   *   *

About this time Town used to swing so gay
When glow-lamps budded in the light blue trees,
And girls glanced lovelier as the air grew dim, –
In the old times, before he threw away his knees.
Now he will never feel again how slim
Girls' waists are, or how warm their subtle hands.
All of them touch him like some queer disease.

*   *   *

There was an artist silly for his face,
For it was younger than his youth, last year.
Now, he is old; his back will never brace;
He's lost his colour very far from here,
Poured it down shell-holes till the veins ran dry,
And half his lifetime lapsed in the hot race
And leap of purple spurted from his thigh.

*   *   *

One time he liked a blood-smear down his leg,
After the matches, carried shoulder-high.
It was after football, when he'd drunk a peg,
He thought he'd better join. – He wonders why.
Someone had said he'd look a god in kilts,
That's why; and maybe, too, to please his Meg,
Aye, that was it, to please the giddy jilts

He asked to join. He didn't have to beg;
Smiling they wrote his lie: aged nineteen years.
Germans he scarcely thought of; all their guilt,
And Austria's, did not move him. And no fears
Of Fear came yet. He thought of jewelled hilts
For daggers in plaid socks; of smart salutes;
And care of arms; and leave; and pay arrears;
Esprit de corps; and hints for young recruits.
And soon, he was drafted out with drums and cheers.

*   *   *

Some cheered him home, but not as crowds cheer Goal.
Only a solemn man who brought him fruits
Thanked him; and then enquired about his soul.

*   *   *

Now, he will spend a few sick years in institutes,
And do what things the rules consider wise,
And take whatever pity they may dole.
Tonight he noticed how the women's eyes
Passed from him to the strong men that were whole.
How cold and late it is! Why don't they come
And put him into bed? Why don't they come?

A Terre

(being the philosophy of many soldiers)

Sit on the bed. I'm blind, and three parts shell.
Be careful; can't shake hands now; never shall.
Both arms have mutinied against me, – brutes.
My fingers fidget like ten idle brats.

I tried to peg out soldierly, – no use!
One dies of war like any old disease.
This bandage feels like pennies on my eyes.
I have my medals? – Discs to make eyes close.
My glorious ribbons? – Ripped from my own back
In scarlet shreds. (That's for your poetry book.)

A short life and a merry one, my buck!
We used to say we'd hate to live dead-old, –
Yet now ... I'd willingly be puffy, bald,
And patriotic. Buffers catch from boys
At least the jokes hurled at them. I suppose
Little I'd ever teach a son, but hitting,
Shooting, war, hunting, all the arts of hurting.
Well, that's what I learnt, – that, and making money.

Your fifty years ahead seem none too many?
Tell me how long I've got? God! For one year
To help myself to nothing more than air!
One Spring! Is one too good to spare, too long?
Spring wind would work its own way to my lung,
And grow me legs as quick as lilac-shoots.

My servant's lamed, but listen how he shouts!
When I'm lugged out, he'll still be good for that.
Here in this mummy-case, you know, I've thought
How well I might have swept his floors for ever.
I'd ask no nights off when the bustle's over,
Enjoying so the dirt. Who's prejudiced

Against a grimed hand when his own's quite dust,
Less live than specks that in the sun-shafts turn,
Less warm than dust that mixes with arms' tan?
I'd love to be a sweep, now, black as Town,
Yes, or a muckman. Must I be his load?

O Life, Life, let me breathe, – a dug-out rat!
Not worse than ours the lives rats lead –
Nosing along at night down some safe rut,
They find a shell-proof home before they rot.
Dead men may envy living mites in cheese,
Or good germs even. Microbes have their joys,
And subdivide, and never come to death.
Certainly flowers have the easiest time on earth,
'I shall be one with nature, herb, and stone,'
Shelley would tell me. Shelley would be stunned:
The dullest Tommy hugs that fancy now.
'Pushing up daisies' is their creed, you know.

To grain, then, go my fat, to buds my sap,
For all the usefulness there is in soap.
D'you think the Boche will ever stew man-soup?
Some day, no doubt, if ...
                                    Friend, be very sure
I shall be better off with plants that share
More peaceably the meadow and the shower.
Soft rains will touch me, – as they could touch once,
And nothing but the sun shall make me ware.
Your guns may crash around me. I'll not hear;
Or, if I wince, I shall not know I wince.

Don't take my soul's poor comfort for your jest.
Soldiers may grow a soul when turned to fronds,
But here the thing's best left at home with friends.

My soul's a little grief, grappling your chest,
To climb your throat on sobs; easily chased
On other sighs and wiped by fresher winds.

Carry my crying spirit till it's weaned
To do without what blood remained these wounds.

The Kind Ghosts

She sleeps on soft, last breaths; but no ghost looms
Out of the stillness of her palace wall,
Her wall of boys on boys and dooms on dooms.

She dreams of golden gardens and sweet glooms,
Not marvelling why her roses never fall
Nor what red mouths were torn to make their blooms.

The shades keep down which well might roam her hall.
Quiet their blood lies in her crimson rooms
And she is not afraid of their footfall.

They move not from her tapestries, their pall,
Nor pace her terraces, their hecatombs,
Lest aught she be disturbed, or grieved at all.

Exposure

Our brains ache, in the merciless iced east winds that knive
    us ...
Wearied we keep awake because the night is silent ...
Low, drooping flares confuse our memory of the salient ...
Worried by silence, sentries whisper, curious, nervous,
        But nothing happens.

Watching, we hear the mad gusts tugging on the wire,
Like twitching agonies of men among its brambles.
Northward, incessantly, the flickering gunnery rumbles,
Far off, like a dull rumour of some other war.
        What are we doing here?

The poignant misery of dawn begins to grow ...
We only know war lasts, rain soaks, and clouds sag stormy.
Dawn massing in the east her melancholy army
Attacks once more in ranks on shivering ranks of grey,
        But nothing happens.

Sudden successive flights of bullets streak the silence.
Less deathly than the air that shudders black with snow,
With sidelong flowing flakes that flock, pause, and renew;
We watch them wandering up and down the wind's
    nonchalance,
        But nothing happens.

Pale flakes with fingering stealth come feeling for our faces –
We cringe in holes, back on forgotten dreams, and stare,
    snow-dazed,
Deep into grassier ditches. So we drowse, sun-dozed,
Littered with blossoms trickling where the blackbird fusses,
        – Is it that we are dying?

Slowly our ghosts drag home: glimpsing the sunk fires, glozed
With crusted dark-red jewels; crickets jingle there;

For hours the innocent mice rejoice: the house is theirs;
Shutters and doors, all closed: on us the doors are closed, –
     We turn back to our dying.

Since we believe not otherwise can kind fires burn;
Nor ever suns smile true on child, or field, or fruit.
For God's invincible spring our love is made afraid;
Therefore, not loath, we lie out here; therefore were born,
     For love of God seems dying.

Tonight, this frost will fasten on this mud and us,
Shrivelling many hands, puckering foreheads crisp.
The burying-party, picks and shovels in shaking grasp,
Pause over half-known faces. All their eyes are ice,
     But nothing happens.

The Sentry

We'd found an old Boche dug-out, and he knew,
And gave us hell; for shell on frantic shell
Lit full on top, but never quite burst through.
Rain, guttering down in waterfalls of slime,
Kept slush waist-high and rising hour by hour,
And choked the steps too thick with clay to climb.
What murk of air remained stank old, and sour
With fumes from whizz-bangs, and the smell of men
Who'd lived there years, and left their curse in the den,
If not their corpses ...

                There we herded from the blast
Of whizz-bangs; but one found our door at last, –
Buffeting eyes and breath, snuffing the candles,
And thud! flump! thud! down the steep steps came thumping
And sploshing in the flood, deluging muck,
The sentry's body; then his rifle, handles
Of old Boche bombs, and mud in ruck on ruck.
We dredged it up, for dead, until he whined,
'O sir – my eyes, – I'm blind, – I'm blind, – I'm blind.'
Coaxing, I held a flame against his lids
And said if he could see the least blurred light
He was not blind; in time they'd get all right.
'I can't,' he sobbed. Eyeballs, huge-bulged like squids',
Watch my dreams still, – yet I forgot him there
In posting Next for duty, and sending a scout
To beg a stretcher somewhere, and flound'ring about
To other posts under the shrieking air.

Those other wretches, how they bled and spewed,
And one who would have drowned himself for good, –
I try not to remember these things now.
Let Dread hark back for one word only: how,
Half-listening to that sentry's moans and jumps,

And the wild chattering of his shivered teeth,
Renewed most horribly whenever crumps
Pummelled the roof and slogged the air beneath, –
Through the dense din, I say, we heard him shout
'I see your lights!' – But ours had long gone out.

Smile, Smile, Smile

Head to limp head, the sunk-eyed wounded scanned
Yesterday's *Mail*; the casualties (typed small)
And (large) Vast Booty from our Latest Haul.
Also, they read of Cheap Homes, not yet planned,
'For', said the paper, 'when this war is done
The men's first instincts will be making homes.
Meanwhile their foremost need is aerodromes,
It being certain war has but begun.
Peace would do wrong to our undying dead, –
The sons we offered might regret they died
If we got nothing lasting in their stead.
We must be solidly indemnified.
Though all be worthy Victory which all bought,
We rulers sitting in this ancient spot
Would wrong our very selves if we forgot
The greatest glory will be theirs who fought,
Who kept this nation in integrity.'
Nation? – The half-limbed readers did not chafe
But smiled at one another curiously
Like secret men who know their secret safe.
(This is the thing they know and never speak,
That England one by one had fled to France,
Not many elsewhere now, save under France.)
Pictures of these broad smiles appear each week,
And people in whose voice real feeling rings
Say: How they smile! They're happy now, poor things.

Spring Offensive

Halted against the shade of a last hill
They fed, and eased of pack-loads, were at ease;
And leaning on the nearest chest or knees
Carelessly slept.
                 But many there stood still
To face the stark blank sky beyond the ridge,
Knowing their feet had come to the end of the world.
Marvelling they stood, and watched the long grass swirled
By the May breeze, murmurous with wasp and midge;
And though the summer oozed into their veins
Like an injected drug for their bodies' pains,
Sharp on their souls hung the imminent ridge of grass,
Fearfully flashed the sky's mysterious glass.

Hour after hour they ponder the warm field
And the far valley behind, where buttercups
Had blessed with gold their slow boots coming up;
When even the little brambles would not yield
But clutched and clung to them like sorrowing arms.
They breathe like trees unstirred.

Till like a cold gust thrills the little word
At which each body and its soul begird
And tighten them for battle. No alarms
Of bugles, no high flags, no clamorous haste, –
Only a lift and flare of eyes that faced
The sun, like a friend with whom their love is done.
O larger shone that smile against the sun, –
Mightier than his whose bounty these have spurned.

So, soon they topped the hill, and raced together
Over an open stretch of herb and heather
Exposed. And instantly the whole sky burned
With fury against them; earth set sudden cups

In thousands for their blood; and the green slope
Chasmed and deepened sheer to infinite space.

Of them who running on that last high place
Breasted the surf of bullets, or went up
On the hot blast and fury of hell's upsurge,
Or plunged and fell away past this world's verge,
Some say God caught them even before they fell.

But what say such as from existence' brink
Ventured but drave too swift to sink,
The few who rushed in the body to enter hell,
And there out-fiending all its fiends and flames
With superhuman inhumanities,
Long-famous glories, immemorial shames –
And crawling slowly back, have by degrees
Regained cool peaceful air in wonder –
Why speak not they of comrades that went under?

Preface

[Draft written by Owen for a collection of war poems he hoped to publish in 1919]

This book is not about heroes. English poetry is not yet fit to speak of them.

Nor is it about deeds, or lands, nor anything about glory, honour, might, majesty, dominion, or power, except War.

Above all I am not concerned with Poetry.

My subject is War, and the pity of War.

The Poetry is in the pity.

Yet these elegies are to this generation in no sense consolatory. They may be to the next. All a poet can do today is warn. That is why the true Poets must be truthful.

(If I thought the letter of this book would last, I might have used proper names; but if the spirit of it survives – survives Prussia – my ambition and those names will have achieved fresher fields than Flanders ....)

Notes

Anthem for Doomed Youth (p. 13) – Owen was probably responding to the anonymous Prefatory Note to *Poems of Today: an Anthology* (1916), of which he possessed the December 1916 reprint: 'This book has been compiled in order that boys and girls, already perhaps familiar with the great classics of the English speech, may also know something of the newer poetry of their own day. Most of the writers are living, and the rest are still vivid memories among us, while one of the youngest, almost as these words are written, has gone singing to lay down his life for his country's cause [...] there is no arbitrary isolation of one theme from another; they mingle and interpenetrate throughout, to the music of Pan's flute, and of Love's viol, and the bugle-call of Endeavour, and the passing-bells of Death.'

'Cramped in that funnelled hole' (p. 19) – Compare Tennyson, 'The Charge of the Light Brigade', ll. 24–6: 'Into the jaws of Death, / Into the mouth of Hell / Rode the six hundred.'

Dulce et Decorum Est (p. 27) – Jessie Pope, to whom the manuscripts of this poem show it was originally to have been dedicated, was the author of numerous pre-war children's books, as well as of *Jessie Pope's War Poems* (1915), *More War Poems* (1915), and *Simple Rhymes for Stirring Times* (1916). Owen might have read (in the *Daily Mail* of 26 November 1914) the disturbing variation of the 'Who's for Tennis' formula offered by her poem 'The Call', beginning:

Who's for the trench –
    Are you, my laddie?
Who'll follow the French –
    Will you, my laddie?
Who's fretting to begin,

Who's going to win?
And who wants to save his skin –
   Do you, my laddie?